COUNTING

FIRST MATHS

©2017
Book Lifc
King's Lynn
Norfolk PE30 4LS

ISBN: 978-1-78637-120-1

Written by:
Joanna Brundle

Designed by:
Danielle Jones

A catalogue record for this book
is available from the British Library

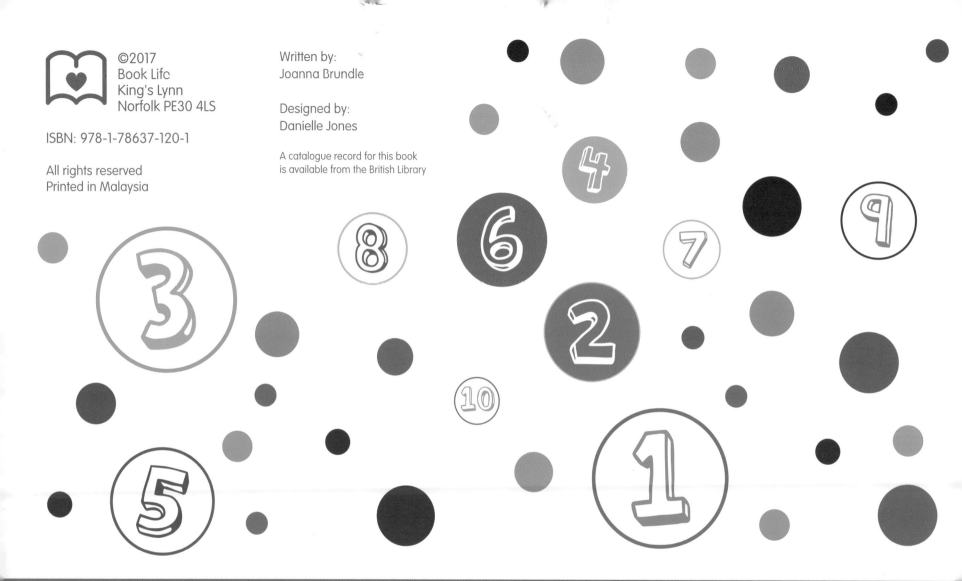

PHOTO CREDITS

CONTENTS

Trace the numbers with your finger as you read.

1

1   2   3

one

One
blue
balloon.

2

two

Two chirpy chicks.

3

1 2 3

three

Three green grapes.

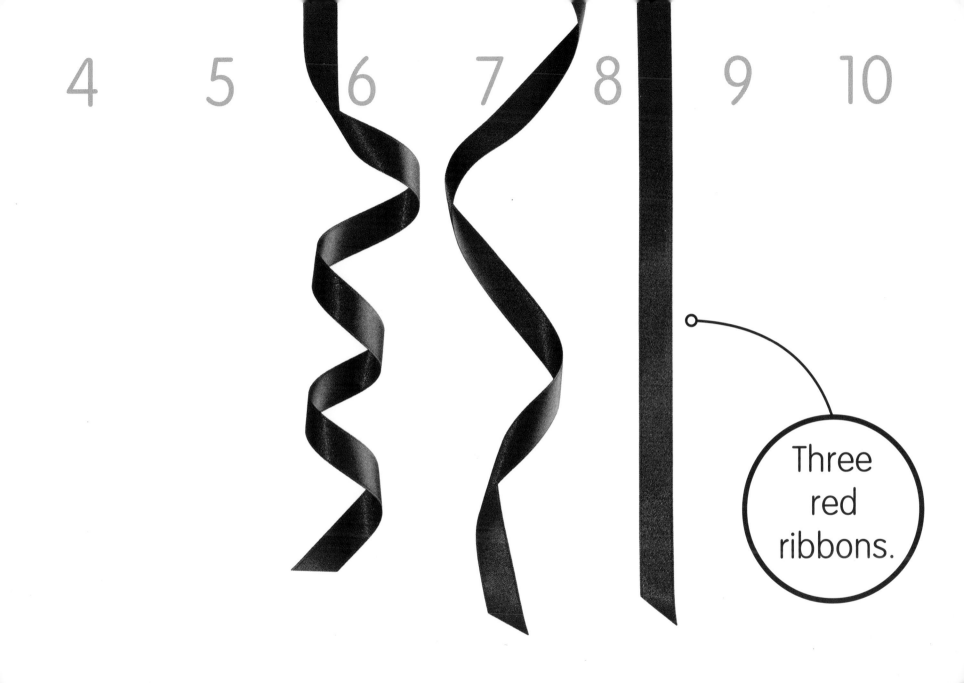

Three red ribbons.

4
four

1   2   3

Four bouncy balls.

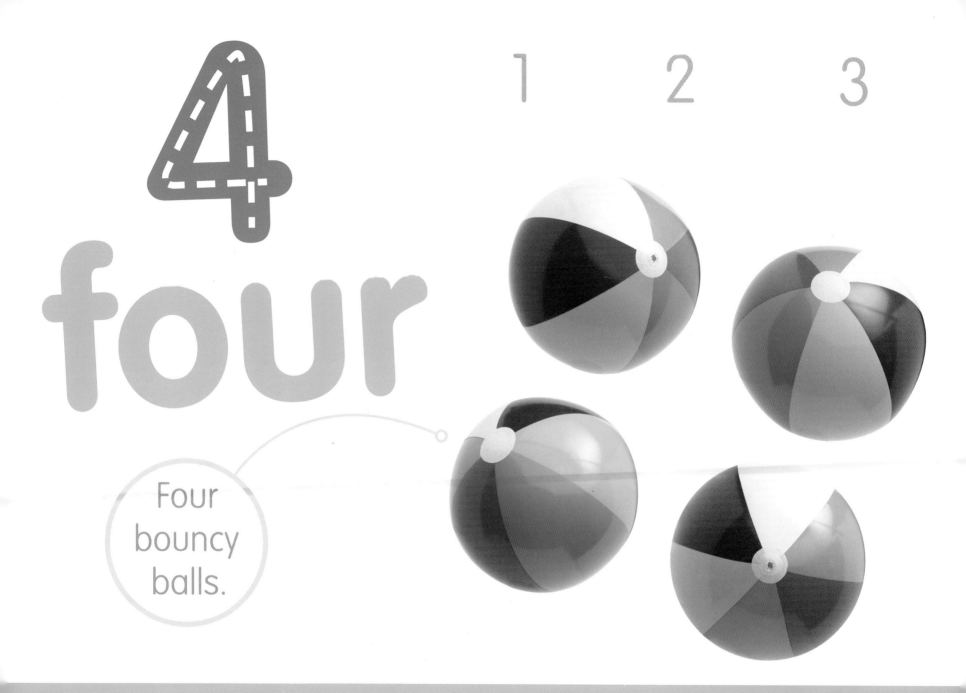

Four cuddly kittens.

5
five

1   2   3

Five crunchy carrots.

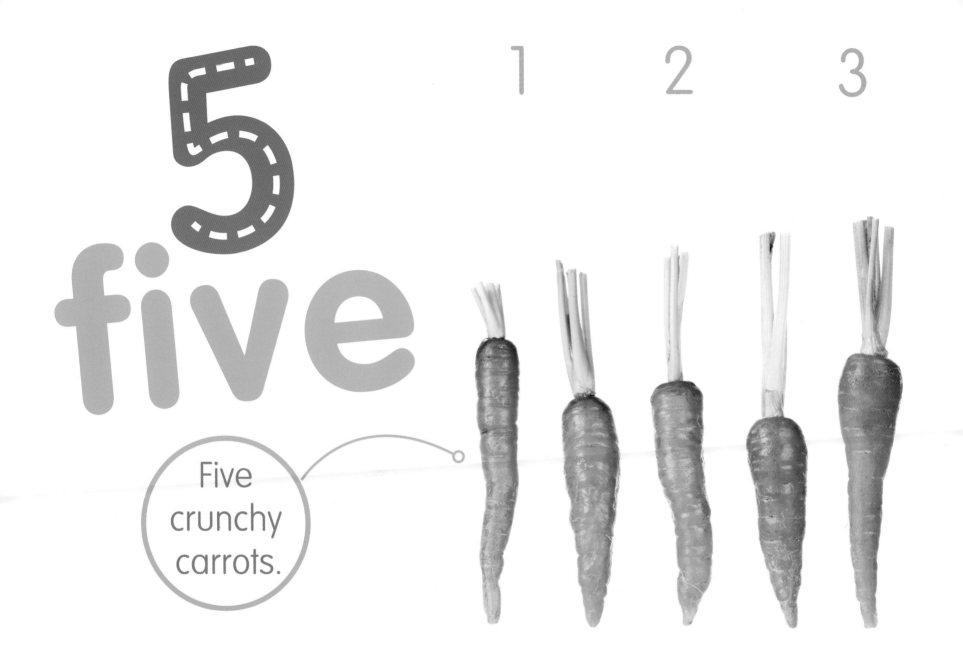

4 **5** 6 7 8 9 10

Five playful puppies.

6

six

1 2 3

Six sizzling sausages.

7 seven

1 2 3

Seven little lambs.

Seven sweet strawberries.

8

eight

Eight floating fish.

1 2 3

9

nine

1 2 3

Nine beautiful butterflies.

4 5 6 7 8 **9** 10

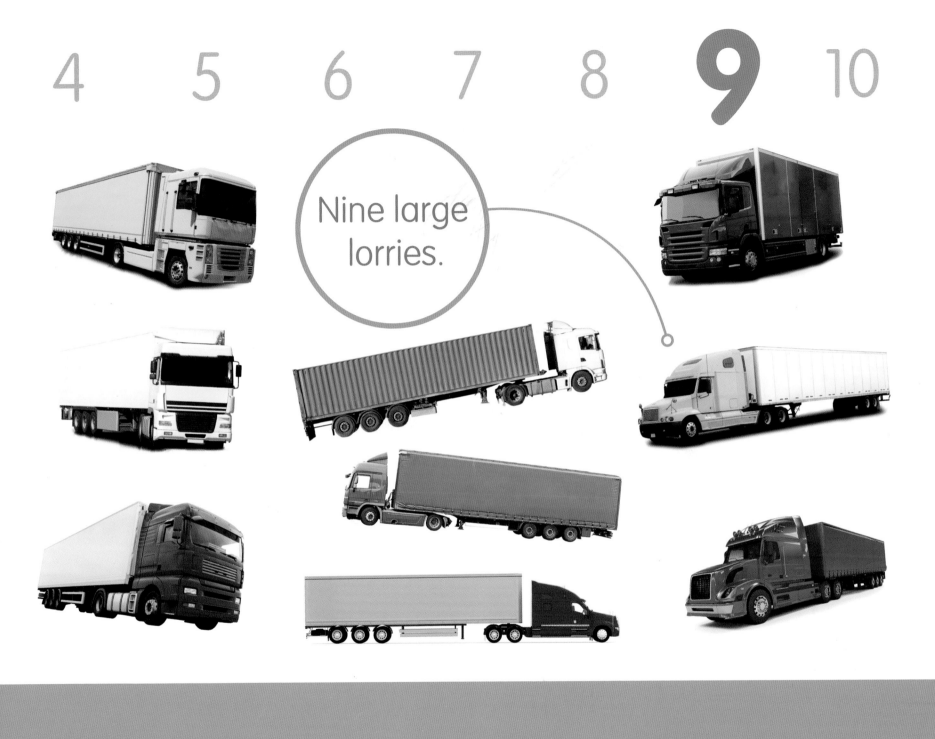

Nine large lorries.

21

10
ten

Ten colourful crayons.

Ten tall trees.

How Many Can You See?

Answers: 3 presents, 6 horses, 10 tractors